CW01651599

A Question of Freedom

Lucy Jane Bledsoe

LEARNING · DEVELOPMENT · AIDS

A Question of Freedom
LD875X
ISBN 1 85503 010 1

Published under licence in the UK by LDA

First published in UK 1990

LDA, Duke Street, Wisbech, Cambs., PE13 2AE England

Printed in Great Britain by Ebenezer Baylis and Son Ltd,
The Trinity Press, Worcester, and London.

CHAPTER

1

The First Lie

Elizabeth's long black hair flew behind her. Beads of sweat ran down her face. She had on her best dress, the red one that Daryl had given her years ago when they were first married. Now its long skirt dragged in the mud as she ran through the woods. Her sleeves kept tearing on tree branches. She gulped for air and tried to run faster.

"Daryl!" Elizabeth screamed, and tripped. She fell to the ground on her hands and knees. She bent over, grabbing her stomach. She could run no more.

But then she heard dogs growling. She also heard the sound of boots pounding through the woods. The sound was getting closer. She had to keep moving and find the river.

Elizabeth struggled to her feet and began to run again. The forest was pitch black. Her heavy dress slowed her down. She fell once again, tripping over a log. She lay in the soft, wet leaves for a moment. But at the sound of barking dogs she dragged herself up again.

Her heart racing with fear, Elizabeth screamed her husband's name again. She jumped over rocks and dodged trees. Finally she saw the muddy water of the McCall River.

Elizabeth's heart now seemed to stop and sink to the bottom of her stomach. She remembered she couldn't swim.

She dived in anyway. Then she heard the first gunshot. Then another. Her legs and arms felt heavy. She was going to drown. She kicked and splashed in the water, gasping for air. Men were shouting at her from the bank of the river. She began to go under. A hand grabbed her. Elizabeth screamed.

"Wake up. Elizabeth! It's me, Daryl! You're having a bad dream. Wake up. Elizabeth. It's all right now."

"Oh, Daryl." Elizabeth let her husband hold her. She was bathed in sweat. So were the sheets on the bed.

"I heard you screaming," Daryl said. "It's all right now, dear. What were you dreaming about?"

Elizabeth was still shaking. Her heart was pounding so hard she thought it would come out of her chest. "I'll be all right now," she was finally able to say. "Let me get up and wash."

"Why don't you just stay in bed a while. You need some rest."

"No, I'll get up. Please, Daryl."

Daryl stood up. He knew that set look on his wife's face. It meant she could not be reasoned with now. He left her alone.

Elizabeth fell back onto the feather pillows and breathed deeply. She wished she could tell Daryl about her dream. She wanted so much to tell him everything. But she needed a few minutes alone to think, to decide what to do.

The dream had to do with what she had heard last night, of course. Yet she couldn't possibly tell Daryl where she had been. Never in a hundred years.

"Oh, what have I done?" Elizabeth moaned out loud. She had never lied to her husband before. Ever! How could she be so foolish. Daryl would see the lie all over her face. He often knew when something was wrong almost before she did.

Elizabeth decided she would just have to put last night out of her mind. She would pretend it never happened.

And she would never do such a thing again. Then it wouldn't really be a lie. It would just be a mistake. And it would be finished.

As Elizabeth brushed her long dark hair, her hands were shaking. She would never be able to forget what she'd learned last night. She felt like she had been changed forever. She felt like a part of herself was being called forward, and she couldn't hold back. Even if it meant the ruin of everything she had lived for up until now – her home, Daryl, and her whole way of life.

Elizabeth knotted her hair at the back of her neck and put on a blue dress. She quietly went downstairs to join Daryl for breakfast.

At the table Daryl was reading the *Maryland Gazette*. Elizabeth picked up part of the newspaper. Everything in the paper reminded her of last night's meeting: Abraham Lincoln, slavery, and war between the states. The Maryland Gazette believed Lincoln might be elected president of the United States. If he were elected, there would surely be a war between the North and the South.

Several southern states were already threatening to leave the Union.

Elizabeth put her head in her hands. All she and Daryl wanted was to live on their farm in peace. But war would surely destroy their lives.

Elizabeth and Daryl Stellar had been married for ten years. Elizabeth could not imagine being any happier. She loved Daryl more than anyone in the world. He was playful, kind, and a wonderful talker. Besides that, he had always respected Elizabeth's choice of friends and activities.

Daryl made a good living as a businessman. They lived on a small farm just outside of Baltimore, Maryland. They bought it shortly after they were married and planned on spending the rest of their lives there.

More than anything else about the farm, Elizabeth loved the garden. Her cousin Martha thought it wasn't ladylike for a woman in her position to dig around in the dirt. But Elizabeth wouldn't let anyone else touch her garden. She loved nothing more than to spend hours planting her favourite flowers.

Elizabeth had always believed that nothing could ever spoil her and Daryl's perfect happiness.

However, dark clouds had been gathering over the South for several years. Now, in 1860, it looked as if the dark clouds might burst. The whole country was being torn apart over the question of slavery. Talk of war was everywhere. Elizabeth and Daryl had said to each other that they would stay out of it. They would let others fight the fights.

After last night, though, Elizabeth was beginning to realise that might not be possible.

Corinn, the Stellars' only servant, set a bowl of fresh fruit and cream in front of Elizabeth. She drank her coffee slowly, but couldn't touch the food.

"I should tell Daryl right now," Elizabeth thought. "Before it becomes a real lie. He will be angry. But I won't ever go there again. It will be over with."

Suddenly Daryl dropped the newspaper and scowled. He began to eat his strawberries.

"Now," Elizabeth said to herself. "Tell him right now."

"Elizabeth."

"Yes?" she said, a little startled when Daryl spoke her name.

"What's the matter?" he asked.

"Oh, nothing, I guess I'm a little nervous because I didn't sleep well."

"Yes, you do look tired. I'm sorry you had a bad night."

"Well, anyway," Daryl went on, "I thought you told me you were going to see Ann last night."

Elizabeth's heart skipped a beat. She had been caught.

"Well, uh . . . yes, I did go to see her."

"I stopped by there on the way home from my meeting. I thought I would walk you home. No one was there."

"Oh, course not." Elizabeth swallowed hard. Was this all he knew? Only that she wasn't at Ann's? She forgot about telling the truth. "We went out for a walk."

"Two women alone?"

"We didn't go far. And really, it wasn't dark yet at 8.30."

"Well, nearly. I don't approve of ladies walking alone at night. Even if some people do."

"Oh, Daryl." Elizabeth smiled, and Daryl smiled back at her. They had a good understanding in their marriage. They both believed that each should have the freedom to grow and explore new ideas and friends. Lying, however, was not part of their understanding.

"All right," Daryl said, still smiling. "I suppose that friend of yours, Ann, is putting more new ideas in your head. Next thing I know, you'll be wearing bloomers."

"Well," Elizabeth said, putting her chin up in the air. "As a matter of fact, I wanted to try on a pair. Don't you think they would be perfect for gardening?"

Daryl just shook his head and laughed a little. He folded the paper and pushed it across the table to Elizabeth. "I've got to get to work early. It's been very busy at the office."

"Will you be home for dinner?"

"I'm not sure."

"Dear, you're working too hard."

"Don't worry, Elizabeth. I'm fine." He kissed her and left the house.

Elizabeth leaned back in her chair and let out a long breath. She was filled with relief. Daryl didn't know where she'd gone last night. And she hadn't really lied to him. She *had* gone to see Ann and they *had* gone for a walk. She'd just left out the part about *where* they'd gone.

Elizabeth's good friend, Ann Williams, had taken her to an abolitionist meeting. The abolitionists were the people working to end slavery in the South. They had helped more than 50,000 slaves escape north to freedom on the "underground railway." That was the name people had given to the swift and secret way the runaway slaves escaped – even though no one ever went underground or went on a train. Helping slaves escape was dangerous work, and it was against the law.

Elizabeth had listened closely at the meeting, and had become deeply disturbed. The idea of people *owning* other people was wrong. Elizabeth had always known that in her heart. And the idea of people *hunting* runaway slaves was terrible. Of course, that was where her bad dream had come from. The speaker at last night's meeting had also read part of the Constitution. It said, "All men are created equal . . . ." He said that meant black people, too.

A part of Elizabeth believed every single word the man said. Even so, white and black people in the South had lived like this for years. It was the normal way of life, the only way of life Elizabeth had ever known. Why were the abolitionists trying to change everything now? Why were they forcing the country into a war between the North and the South?

Elizabeth knew she had no business even thinking about this question. Daryl's whole job depended on slavery. His company exported products from the South. These were farm products that slaves harvested from the fields. Imagine what he would say if he knew his wife had gone to an abolitionist meeting!

"He will never know," Elizabeth said to herself. "I will not even think about these things anymore."

"May I take your breakfast dishes?"

Elizabeth jumped and swung around. "Oh, Corinn. I didn't now you were in the room. You frightened me."

"I'm sorry, ma'am."

"I've finished with breakfast," Elizabeth said. Then she added, though she never had before, "Thank you."

Elizabeth was glad that she and Daryl had only one slave. Besides, Elizabeth hardly thought of Corinn as a slave, anyway. Corinn had been in the family for as long as Elizabeth could remember. Corinn and Elizabeth had been born in the same year. The girls played together when they were children. When they grew older, they were kept apart. That was how things were in the South.

When Elizabeth married Daryl, her father sent Corinn to live with them. Elizabeth was delighted.

Elizabeth knew that Corinn was a serious and quiet woman who would never cause trouble. Elizabeth was certain that Corinn was as happy in their home as she and Daryl were.

CHAPTER

2

Corinn's Visitor

That afternoon Elizabeth's reading club was going to meet at her house. Ann Williams, Elizabeth's cousin, Martha Murphy, and their friend Priscilla Thompson were in the group. The four women used to have a pleasant time reading, talking, and sewing. But lately all they seemed to do was argue. It all started a year ago when they read that best-seller, *Uncle Tom's Cabin*. It was written by an abolitionist named Harriet Beecher Stowe. The ideas in the book caused the women to think a lot about the issue of slavery. And it had caused some hard feelings.

"Corinn," Elizabeth called on her way to the kitchen. "We'll only need coffee this afternoon. I think I'll make my cinnamon rolls."

"I can make the rolls, ma'am." Corinn said.

Elizabeth was surprised. She always made the cinnamon rolls. She used an old family recipe. "That's all right, Corinn. I'm looking forward to making them," she said.

Corinn glanced at the pantry. "What do you need from the pantry? Flour and what else? I'll get it."

"Really, Corinn. Don't you have the dusting and cleaning to do? I'll take care of this."

Elizabeth had a puzzled look on her face as she watched Corinn leave the room. It was unlike Corinn to not know just what was expected of her.

Elizabeth shrugged and went to the kitchen. Her cousin Martha also thought the kitchen was no place for a lady. Elizabeth laughed a little thinking of Martha. The two women had grown up on neighbouring farms, and had been best friends since they could walk. They had spent hours riding horses and climbing trees with their brothers and the slave children.

The difference between Martha and Elizabeth was that Martha had outgrown the children's games. Elizabeth had never outgrown adventure. That was something that Martha couldn't accept. She had always taken it upon herself to let Elizabeth know how she should act. Elizabeth usually just laughed it off.

Lately, the differences between the two of them had become a bit more serious. But Martha was family. Elizabeth did her best to ignore their differences.

Elizabeth carried two bowls to the pantry. She filled one with raisins. The other bowl was for the flour. But when she took the top off the flour barrel, she saw that it was nearly empty. How strange, she thought. She was sure she had bought a barrel not long ago. She looked in the cornmeal barrel, and it, too, was low. She supposed she and Daryl had been eating at home a lot more often lately.

Just as she was finishing the cinnamon rolls, there was a knock at the kitchen door. Elizabeth knew what Martha would say about the lady of the house answering the kitchen door! But Corinn was upstairs dusting. Elizabeth pulled open the door.

A tall, good-looking black man stood with a bunch of flowers in his hand. She recognised him as Jonathan, a slave on a farm outside the town.

Jonathan looked startled when he saw Elizabeth. He certainly had not expected *her* to answer the door.

"I'm sorry, ma'am. I, well –"

"Are you delivering something?" Elizabeth asked.

"No, ma'am," Jonathan said, holding his flowers tightly. The two stood staring at each other, not knowing what to do. It was clear to Elizabeth that Jonathan had been sent to town to do something for his master. He had taken the opportunity to stop and give these flowers to Corinn. She also knew that this side trip would be cause for punishment if his master found out about it.

Elizabeth remembered seeing Corinn talking with Jonathan in town once or twice before. She had wondered then if there was something between them. But she had never asked Corinn about it. Maybe she should have.

Elizabeth now looked at the tall man before her, and tried to decide what to do next. She was supposed to act angry. She should tell him she did not want to see him on their property again. But Elizabeth simply couldn't. She was touched by the flowers. She wanted Corinn to have them.

She tried to cover up her softer feelings by speaking sternly. She said, "I suppose those are for Corinn."

"Well, yes, ma'am."

"Give them to me. I'll see that she gets them."

Jonathan became nervous. His hands were shaking and he began to step backwards. "Well, thank you, ma'am, but I don't . . . ." Elizabeth reached for the flowers.

Jonathan yanked the flowers back. He moved so fast the whole bunch slipped in his hand and loosened. A piece of paper went fluttering from the centre of the flowers to the ground.

Jonathan jumped after the paper as if it was a hundred-dollar bill. Then he turned and left quickly, taking his note and flowers, without saying another word.

Elizabeth shut the kitchen door slowly. She had a feeling that something odd was going on. There were plenty of reasons Jonathan might have been frightened. He could have thought Elizabeth would tell his master he had come here. Or, that she would read the note. Or even punish Corinn. Even so, there was something more in Jonathan's face. It was something Elizabeth could not quite put her finger on.

She decided not to mention Jonathan's visit, either to Corinn or to Daryl. She continued to get ready for her reading group.

CHAPTER

3

Runaway Slaves

Everything was ready by the time the first guest arrived. Elizabeth hoped the knock at the door was Ann. But when Corinn showed the guest into the drawing room, it was Priscilla. Priscilla wore a fancy, full dress that was covered with flowers. "She always overdresses," thought Elizabeth.

"Wasn't the meeting last night exciting!" Priscilla squealed right away. "I thought the speaker was so good-looking, didn't you? Too bad he's a minister!" Priscilla giggled and took off her gloves.

"Priscilla!" Elizabeth said glancing nervously at Corinn.

"Oh!" Priscilla slapped a hand over her mouth. "I should learn to be more careful."

"Things are getting bad," Elizabeth thought, "if I have to hide my activities from Corinn."

When Corinn had left the room, Elizabeth said, "I didn't mean to snap at you, Priscilla. But you know the abolitionist meetings are . . . well, it's dangerous to be there. Even the public ones like last night. Please don't mention to anyone else that I was there. I will not be going to another meeting."

"You won't? But how can you stay away from that good-looking minister? Those blue eyes are too much for me!" Priscilla put two cinnamon rolls on a plate. "These look *sooo* good."

Elizabeth was relieved when the bell rang again and Ann came in. Next to Daryl, Ann was her most favourite person of all. She was wearing a simple blue dress and had a serious look on her face.

"Well, have you thought it over?" Ann asked her two friends right away. "Do you think you will be able to do some work for us?"

"You can count on me," Priscilla said. Then she giggled. "As long as that minister is part of the group."

"Elizabeth?" Ann took her friend's hand.

"Ann, I admire the work you are doing so much. But you know Daryl's business is all tied up with slavery. How could I? I'm sorry. I've already gone too far."

Ann stepped back. She looked disappointed. "All right. But I want to warn you about one thing. I don't think we should talk about this in front of Martha anymore."

"Why not?" Priscilla asked.

"I know she doesn't hold our – well, *my* – point of view," Ann said. "And it's just not safe anymore with –"

Ann cut herself off quickly when she noticed Corinn. She had come in silently with a fresh pot of coffee and was standing in a corner waiting to pour it.

"We still have plenty of coffee," Elizabeth said to her. Just then the bell rang, and Corinn left to answer it.

Martha burst into the room. "Well! The worst has happened," she nearly shouted. Her face was red with anger.

"What?" asked Elizabeth.

"Three of our slaves ran away last night!" Martha said. She threw an angry look toward Corinn.

"Oh, my gosh," Priscilla said in a high-pitched voice.

Elizabeth remained silent. She looked around at her friends. Priscilla was on the edge of her chair. Ann was studying her nails. Martha was throwing her hat and coat on a chair.

"We have $1000 out on each of the men and $700 on the woman," Martha said. "I am so angry. And people like you, Ann, are encouraging it." She pointed a finger.

"You know how I feel, Martha," Ann said. "There's no use getting into it."

"No use getting into it! Did you hear that, Elizabeth?" Martha yanked off her gloves. She always tried to get Elizabeth to take her side. "I think you'd feel different if you lost thousands of dollars worth of property."

"You haven't," Ann said quietly.

"Haven't what?" Priscilla asked.

"It is impossible for a human being to be the property of someone else," Ann said. "You talk as if you can put a price tag on someone's head. As if a person were a cow or a horse!"

"I don't know how far you've gone with those abolitionists," Martha said, her voice deep and shaking. "But there was a time when you had more sense. For your own good, I would like to remind you of the law. You can be fined a good deal of money – and even thrown into jail – for helping runaway slaves."

"Thank you for informing me of the law," Ann said hotly.

"You know," Martha said, shaking her finger at Ann. "You think you are so above us all. But think about the facts. A slave has harvested most of the food you eat. A slave has picked the cotton that your fine dresses are made from. That's the way this country works."

"Oh, please," Elizabeth said. "Let's get to talking about this week's book. There is no need for arguing. Martha, I'm sorry about . . . ."

Both Martha and Ann eyed her sharply. She knew that each expected her to take their own side. Elizabeth never finished her sentence.

A few nights later, Elizabeth and Daryl were enjoying a quiet evening at home. Daryl's work had been keeping him at the office late almost every night. Elizabeth was happy to have him at home early for once.

After dinner, they settled in the drawing room with coffee. Daryl was his old self, telling her funny stories about people in his office.

These were Elizabeth's happiest times. She had just begun telling Daryl her new plans for the back garden. Suddenly, there was a loud banging on the door.

"I'll get it," Daryl said. Elizabeth followed him to the door.

"Hello!" called Brian Murphy, Martha's husband. He was a stocky man with small brown eyes. Elizabeth looked from his face down to his hands. Her eyes locked on the long, shiny barrel of a gun.

"Good evening," Daryl said. It was then that Elizabeth saw the shapes of several men standing in the dark behind Brian. As her eyes got used to the dark, she saw that they all had guns. One man had two dogs on a leash.

"Listen, we're putting together a committee," Brian Murphy said. "You probably heard we lost three slaves a few days ago. The Smiths lost five last night," Brian jerked his thumb at Lane Smith, the man holding the dogs. "Seems as if the underground railroad goes right through here. Runaway slaves have been passing through right under our noses." His eyes narrowed.

"What do you want from us?" Elizabeth stepped up next to Daryl.

"We're out to catch the slaves or the folks helping them. Either way, there's big reward money." Brian smiled.

"It's time we took this matter into our own hands," Smith added. "It's time to fight back."

"We thought you might want to help out," Brian Murphy said.

"I'm sorry, but this has nothing to do with us. We can't help you." Daryl said. He started to close the door. Brian put his big boot in the way.

"Yes?" Daryl asked.

"Do you know who Harriet Tubman is?"

"Yes, we've read about her. She's the runaway slave that has been helping a lot of other slaves escape."

"That's right. And do you know what the price is on her head?"

Elizabeth thought of what Ann would say. How can you put a price tag on the head of a human being.

"Look –" Daryl began, trying to shut the door again. He didn't care if Brian Murphy was family. He wasn't going to have a group of gun-carrying men on his doorstep.

But Brian's foot was still in the door. "Forty thousand dollars. That's how much. And that's how serious this is getting. You may think you can stay out of it. But no one can anymore. Everyone has to take sides. If Lincoln gets elected later this year, there's sure to be war. I know where I'll be. Where are you going to stand, Stellar?"

"Look, I'm not interested in running around looking for slaves with guns and dogs," Daryl said. "You think we're keeping runaways here? You want to look through my house? Go ahead. Just leave your guns and dogs outside."

"And your dirty boots," Elizabeth added, her voice cracking with anger.

Brian looked back at the men with him. Smith shrugged. Brian shrugged, too. "No," he said. "We don't think you're hiding runaways here. But keep your ears open. There's big money for any leads that help with the capture of runaways. How about that girl of yours. What's her name? Corinn. She may be in on something."

"Corinn?" Daryl laughed softly. "It's not possible."

"Never." Elizabeth backed him up.

"Don't be too sure," Brian said. "You may want to question her. Let her know you know what's been going on around here. Well, good-night. Sorry to have disturbed your evening."

"They're going too far," Daryl said after shutting the door. "Hunting people for a reward! What are people coming to today?"

Elizabeth agreed. But if that were going too far, where did it stop? What part of slavery was *not* going too far, she wondered.

Brian Murphy was right about one thing. Sooner or later, everyone had to take sides. It looked more and more like a war was coming between the North and South. Elizabeth did not want to have to take sides. But after all, they *were* Southerners. They were even slave owners.

Elizabeth's evening with Daryl had been ruined. After the men left, Daryl slipped into complete silence. Lately, he had been strangely distant and quiet much of the time. Elizabeth wondered if he still loved her as much as he used to . He hardly ever told her what was on his mind anymore.

Elizabeth lay awake in bed that night. She was afraid to sleep for fear of having more bad dreams. She could not stop thinking about the dogs and shiny barrels of the guns. Worst of all, though, was the look on Brian's face. He looked almost as if he were playing a game he enjoyed.

Elizabeth lay awake for a long time listening to the silent night. Then, at about three in the morning, she thought she heard something. She sat up in bed to listen more carefully.

There it was again. Footsteps downstairs.

It must be Daryl, she decided. He probably couldn't sleep, either. Perhaps he got up to make himself a sandwich. Elizabeth got out of bed. She thought she'd make a cup of tea and keep Daryl company.

Elizabeth walked quietly out of her bedroom into the hall. The door to Daryl's bedroom was open. She tiptoed up to it. Daryl made a small mountain in the middle of the bed. He was breathing as softly as a baby.

Elizabeth froze. Then who was downstairs? She started to wake Daryl, but then stopped herself. She was probably just imagining the footsteps. After all, she had been imagining all kinds of crazy things lately.

Of course, it was all in her head. She had been worrying too much. She would go downstairs right now. A cup of tea would calm her. And she would prove to herself, once and for all, that she was just imagining things.

Elizabeth crept down the stairs, one step at a time. Her insides felt as if they were made of jelly.

At the kitchen door, she stopped. Someone *was* there. She heard him plainly now. Elizabeth took a deep breath and threw open the kitchen door.

"Corinn!" Elizabeth could not believe her eyes. Corinn was fully dressed, and had several apples in her apron. "What in the world are you doing?"

Corinn looked as calm as ever. Her eyes were steady and clear. She said, "I was worried, ma'am. I started to think I had left the top off the sugar barrel. You know how bad the ants can be. I thought it would terrible if they got in the sugar."

"You got up in the middle of the night to see if you put the top on the sugar barrel?"

"Yes, ma'am."

"But what are you doing with all those apples?"

"I'm sorry. I got hungry."

Elizabeth stared at Corinn. She knew this was a lie. And she knew that Corinn knew she knew. The apples were for someone else. Too many thoughts were crowding Elizabeth's head at once. She pushed them away. She didn't want to know. Softly, she said,"Corinn, you had better be careful."

Then Elizabeth turned around and left the kitchen.

CHAPTER

4

Frederick Douglass

The next morning Elizabeth put on a hat and her new bloomers. She was going to put five new rose plants in the backyard. She hoped that would take her mind off the strange things that were happening.

The day was clear and blue, perfect for gardening. But as she entered the garden, she stopped short. She heard a noise near the small garden cottage where Corinn lived.

"That's funny," she thought. She had sent Corinn to town a few minutes ago. Elizabeth looked around slowly. Then, feeling braver than last night, she walked quietly towards the cottage.

She saw the back of a woman crouched at one of the windows. The woman's hands were cupped around her face as she looked in.

"Hello?" Elizabeth called to the woman's back.

"What!" the woman cried, jumping up. "Oh! Elizabeth . . . I was . . ."

"Martha!" Elizabeth stepped closer. "Whatever are you doing?"

Martha brushed off her dress and patted her hair. Then she put on a smile. "How silly of me. I know you had been talking about doing something special to the back garden. And since I was out on a walk, I came to see what you had done. I would have come to the door if it weren't so early. I'm sorry. Did I frighten you?"

"No," Elizabeth said. "But why are you looking in Corinn's cottage?"

"This is Corinn's room?" Martha's face was all innocence. "I thought it was your garden room. It's such a good house for a servant. Why did you ever give her such lovely quarters?"

Martha was quick. Elizabeth decided not to ask any more questions. It would do no good. Besides, she wasn't hiding any runaways, so what difference did it make? Let Martha sniff around all she wanted.

"As for the flower beds," Elizabeth said. "I'm just beginning them this morning."

"You really should get a man to do your gardening. It's terrible on your hands. Daryl is certainly able to pay someone."

"I like to do it," Elizabeth said. She turned her back to Martha and picked up the shovel.

"My goodness, what have you got around your legs, Elizabeth!"

"Bloomers," Elizabeth said coldly.

"Well!" Martha waited for Elizabeth to say more. When she didn't, Martha said, "I'll see you at the reading club next week, then. Remember, it's at my house."

This time Martha left through the front of the house. On her way out, she passed Ann, who was coming in.

Ann said to Elizabeth, "I didn't know you were having company this morning."

"I didn't either," Elizabeth answered. She pushed the shovel in the ground with extra force.

"Are you okay?" Ann asked.

"Yes, I'm fine, thank you." Elizabeth leaned the shovel against the house. She calmed down and smiled at Ann.

"I came to tell you about something really exciting," Ann said. "Frederick Douglass is speaking in town! Can you believe it? He'll be there this afternoon. You must come with me. This is something not to miss."

"I can't," Elizabeth said. "You know that. I can't risk being seen in a crowd of abolitionists again. It might ruin Daryl's job." Elizabeth spoke the words as if they were forced on her. She wanted to go, very much. But she had to stay out of it. Her husband's job was not the only thing at risk. Her marriage was also at risk. That was too much to risk giving up.

"No," Elizabeth said out loud, more to herself than to Ann. "I simply can't."

"I'm trying to understand," Ann said. "I know how hard this must be for you."

"Thank you," Elizabeth said. "I wish . . . I wish it were different."

When Daryl came home for lunch he looked as if his mind were elsewhere. Elizabeth told him about the roses she had planted. He didn't even smile.

"I'm afraid I won't be home this evening, Elizabeth," he said as he finished eating. "I have to take the two o'clock train to Washington. My meeting will run too late to get back home tonight."

Elizabeth kept herself from saying, "Again?" She was tired of Daryl being away from home so much.

When Daryl left the house, Elizabeth went upstairs. She sat in her room thinking about how much Daryl had changed in the past few months. He used to be so full of fun all the time. That was what she loved most about him. Lately, he had become so serious. He looked as if he were always troubled by something.

Of course, Elizabeth told herself, it was the election. That was on everyone's mind. If Lincoln were elected, if there were war, Daryl's business could be ruined.

"It's not me," Elizabeth said out loud."He's being so quiet because of *other* troubles." She wanted to believe that. Even so, it was not like Daryl to not talk with her about his problems. Elizabeth stood and walked the length of the room. She turned and walked back. She felt restless. Her thoughts turned to Ann going to hear Frederick Douglass speak. Then she pictured her husband safely on the train to Washington.

Suddenly, Elizabeth ran downstairs. She put on her hat and coat. Next thing she knew, she was out the door.

She hurried along the streets of Baltimore, looking around nervously. She nodded to people she knew. Did they know where she was going? Perhaps they would mention to

Daryl that they had seen her. Even worse, maybe Martha was following her. She did not know whom she could trust any more.

She got the the church just as Frederick Douglass took the speaker's stand. Ann spied her right away and a big smile came across her face. Elizabeth worked her way through the crowd to Ann's side. Her friend hugged her.

Frederick Douglass spoke about how he had run away to his own freedom. He spoke beautifully, and Elizabeth was deeply moved.

Yet even as she listened, she remembered the committee of angry men at their door a few nights ago. She remembered reading about newspaper writers who had been tarred and feathered for writing abolitionist stories. Perhaps there was a price on her very own head – just for being at this meeting!

At the same time, she thought of Daryl in Washington. She had gone with him once to that city. She shivered just remembering it. Washington had the biggest slave market in the country. Right before her eyes people had been made to stand up on blocks. Slave owners yelled out prices, as if these people were cattle. Broken-hearted children were sold away from their mothers and fathers.

Elizabeth had seen nothing like it before. She had told Daryl she would never go with him to Washington again.

"I appear before you," Douglass was saying, "as a thief and a robber. I stole this head, these arms and legs, this body from my master, and ran away with them." Then he asked the crowd, "Is this Negro before you a man or a thing?"

Elizabeth had planned on leaving right after Douglass finished speaking. But when it was over, Ann grabbed hold of her arm. She started to lead her over to the group of people talking with the abolitionist minister.

Elizabeth knew there was no turning back now. These people were doing what was right.

Elizabeth did not see Daryl until lunch the next day. As usual, he looked as if there were a lot of things on his mind. Elizabeth did not seem to be one of them.

"How was Washington?" she asked.

"Oh well, a mess, really. The country is so close to war, and the president isn't doing anything."

"Any news of the election?"

"No. But Lincoln sounds stronger all the time."

"Do you think," she said, changing the subject, "we might have the evening together tonight?"

"I'm sorry. I'm not sure how long I'll have to be at the office." He didn't even look at her as he said this. Then he finished his lunch quickly and left the house.

Elizabeth was growing worried. Perhaps Daryl was getting tired of her. Maybe he was bored with their marriage. Or maybe . . . she could hardly finish the thought. Maybe he cared for someone else.

That afternoon Corinn showed a man into the drawing room. He wore a worn-out overcoat and had a thick beard. His head was covered with a large, funny-looking hat. Elizabeth threw a sharp look at Corinn. Why hadn't she told the man to wait at the door and then come and fetched her?

When Elizabeth asked the man how she could help him, he said, "I'd like to speak to you alone." Elizabeth nodded to Corinn. She didn't know who this man was. But she was not afraid of him.

As soon as Corinn left the room, the man took off his coat and hat. Elizabeth looked nervously at the door. She had not invited him to stay.

Then he began tearing off his beard! Standing before her was the abolitionist minister.

"I don't mean to alarm you," he said softly. "I'm so sorry to come this way. But I thought it was necessary. My name is David Sawyer."

"Yes, I know your name," Elizabeth said. "What do you want?"

"We need your help"

'Help? I'm sorry, but –"

David Sawyer held up a hand. "Hear me out. Please. I know from two people that you can be trusted."

"*Two,*" thought Elizabeth. Certainly Ann was one. But who might the other be? No one else knew her thoughts except, maybe . . .

"The slave hunters are on the trail of three runaways," the minister explained. "They are not safe where they are now. Even as we speak, they are in great danger. They have nowhere to go. The next station is no longer safe, either."

"I could get some food together, if that would help," Elizabeth said. "Or maybe even some clothing. I can do that, but that's all."

The minister took Elizabeth's hand and moved a step closer. "You must let these three people stay in your barn tonight. Because of your husband's position, no one will be suspicious."

"Oh, sir! That is impossible. I understand your commitment to this cause, Mr. Sawyer. I have even come to believe your cause is right and just. But you're asking me to risk not only my safety, but my husband's business and – "

"Ma'am, will you excuse me if I am bold?" the minister cut in. "I am talking about three *lives*. At this minute these people are being tracked by dogs and men with guns. You say you believe our cause is just. Then you *must* help us. I don't believe you will be in great danger. No one would think of looking for these runaways in your barn. It is only for one night. They will be gone tomorrow."

Elizabeth stood up from the chair. She walked across to the bookshelf and turned around. She looked the man squarely in the face. She knew he was right. If she really believed in the abolitionist movement, how could she not agree to help?

"All right," she said quietly. "I will do what I can."

"You're a brave woman, Mrs. Stellar."

"Oh, no, not so brave. I'm as frightened as I've ever been in my life." Elizabeth shook her head. "What do I have to do?"

David Sawyer spoke in a low voice. He told her every part of the plan. When he finished, he paused for a moment. Then he said, "There is something else, Mrs. Stellar. Corinn will be leaving with the group. You must act very surprised when the word gets out. If you must say anything, tell people you are angry. But don't overdo it. Be careful and talk as little as possible. And don't tell your husband a thing."

"But, how can I –" Elizabeth whispered.

"I must go now," the minister said, before she could finish. "Follow my instructions as closely as you possibly can."

Then he put his coat back on. He put the fake beard back on his face, and pulled the hat over his head. Elizabeth showed him to the door.

CHAPTER

5

A Candle in the Window

"At least Daryl will not be home tonight," Elizabeth thought. "Thank goodness for that."

She tried to keep away from Corinn for the rest of the day. She didn't know which was stronger: her admiration for, or her anger at Corinn. She was a brave woman. Elizabeth had to give her that. But why did she want to run away? They had been together their whole lives. Wasn't Corinn happy in their home? Even as Elizabeth asked these questions, she knew the answer. Corinn might be happy living in their home. But it wasn't a question of happiness. It was a question of freedom.

Finally, late in the afternoon, they bumped into each other in the hall.

"Ma'am?" Corinn said.

"I didn't say anything." Elizabeth said sharply.

Corinn started for the kitchen. Elizabeth called her back. It was stupid to pretend that nothing was going on.

"Corinn," she said. "We may as well get some food together. That is, if you haven't done it already. Make some corn bread and chicken. And get some apples, too."

"Ma'am?"

"Yes?"

"What about your husband?"

"Don't worry. Mr. Stellar won't be home until late tonight."

"Did I hear my name?"

Both women turned around to see Daryl entering the hall.

"You're home early!" Elizabeth nearly shouted.

Daryl looked a little puzzled, but then he smiled. "You sound disappointed," he said. "I thought I would surprise you. I brought my work home for the evening."

"Oh, no. I mean, that's wonderful. I'm so glad." How Elizabeth had longed for Daryl to surprise her like this. But not tonight! "I was just telling Corinn you wouldn't be home for supper," she said. "But now you are. So she can make corn bread and chicken."

Elizabeth felt her face turning red. She wondered how much of the earlier conversation Daryl had heard. Had he heard only his name? Of all the nights for him to come home early!

The rest of the afternoon went by quickly. When they sat down to dinner, Elizabeth found that she could not eat. Twice her knife slipped from her hand and crashed on the plate.

"What's wrong, Elizabeth?" Daryl asked. "You seem so nervous."

"I'm not well, I suppose."

"You should go to bed then. Here, let me help you upstairs."

"No!" she said too loudly and quickly. "I mean, I really want to stay up for a while. I'm not tired. My head hurts, that's all."

"As you please." Daryl's face looked tight and drawn.

"Tell me," Elizabeth began, trying to smooth out the tension between them. "Is anything happening at the office?"

"Not so much really. Did you hear about Brian Murphy?"

"No."

"He caught five runaway slaves. That brought him a $3500 reward. And he picked up some extra money for turning in the folks that were hiding them."

"When?" she asked. She wondered if these were the slaves who were supposed to be coming to their barn tonight.

"Yesterday," Daryl said.

Elizabeth was relieved. It was a different group. Suddenly she remembered Martha Murphy looking around her backyard the other morning. Maybe Martha had known more about Corinn than Elizabeth had at the time. Maybe she should have mentioned Martha's nosing around to the minister.

Elizabeth just wanted the night to be over.

"I don't approve at all," Daryl went on to say. "What a way to make a living, slithering around like a snake. All this just so Martha can buy more furs."

"I think it's awful, too," Elizabeth answered. Her voice came out high and thin.

"They say there's a lot of money in it," Daryl went on. "More and more people are taking up slave chasing as if it were a sport." Daryl rubbed his head. Elizabeth noticed how tired he looked.

"I'll be up late tonight," Daryl said. He wiped his mouth with his napkin and started to leave the table.

Elizabeth knew it was time to start following the minister's instructions. She said "I'm going to send Corinn over to Ann's tonight. Ann is quite ill with a bad cold and fever. Corinn is so good at making special teas."

"That's a nice idea. I hope Ann gets well soon."

"Daryl, I was thinking that maybe you should write a note for Corinn. You know how things are now. It's not so safe for a slave to be out at night. But if she has a note from you saying where she is going, she will be all right."

"Oh, yes, of course," Daryl said. "That's a good idea. I'll do it right now."

Daryl left, and Elizabeth let out a long breath. Daryl bought the whole story. Elizabeth was surprised at how easy it was getting to lie to him.

Elizabeth saw Corinn to the door with her note and a large, full basket of food. "Be safe," Elizabeth whispered to her. "Wait for the candle, no matter how late."

"Thank you, ma'am," Corinn said. Then the serious young woman smiled, something

Elizabeth almost never saw her do. Elizabeth shut the door wondering how many people helped their own slaves run away.

The evening hours passed far too slowly. Elizabeth caught up on her sewing. Then she went to bed, so Daryl would not be suspicious.

"I'll be up for a time," were his last words to her.

The hardest part was trying to stay awake as she lay in her bed. Sleep would be such sweet relief. In her mind, Elizabeth went over every step Corinn and the others were taking. She prayed they were safe.

From Ann's house, Corinn would go to the woods. There she would meet the three runaways. She would lead them through the woods to the edge of the Stellars' farm. They would wait in the darkness of the forest until they got the sign from Elizabeth that all was clear.

Finally, at midnight, Elizabeth heard Daryl go to bed. She waited another half hour for him to fall asleep. Then she crept out of bed. She tiptoed to his door and listened. He was breathing evenly, sleeping.

Only one more step to go.

Elizabeth took a candle from her bedroom. She carried it to a back room that had a window facing the woods. Elizabeth carefully placed the burning candle in the window and stepped back. She imagined Corinn and the others stepping out of the woods into the field. Even without a moon, they could be seen in the starlight if anyone were watching. She imagined them moving quietly and quickly to the safety of the barn.

Elizabeth climbed back in her bed almost relieved. She had done her part. The runaways would have a good dinner and a safe night. By morning they would be gone.

She had begun to fall off to sleep when a shocking thought came to her. No one had told her how or when the group was going to leave the barn. And no one had told her where they were going to go.

Elizabeth awoke later that night. She opened her eyes. A figure was moving from the door to her bed. "Daryl?" she whispered.

"No, ma'am," came back another whisper. "It's me."

"Corinn? What is it? Is something wrong?"

"No. But please come out to the barn. We need your help."

"I can't do that! What if Daryl wakes up?"

"We'll have to be very quiet." The two women were speaking in whispers.

"Very well," Elizabeth said. As she brushed sleep from her eyes, she felt stronger. "Daryl sleeps soundly. But if he wakes up, I'll tell him I felt ill and called for you. I'll say you are going to make some tea and run me a bath."

"Yes, ma'am," Corinn said.

The two women moved slowly and quietly through the upstairs hall. A loud groan came from Daryl's room. Then the sound of covers being thrown back.

"Elizabeth?" he called out.

"Yes, dear?" Elizabeth said.

"What are you doing up?"

She told him the story she and Corinn had agreed upon.

"Shall I call for a doctor?" Daryl asked.

"No, I'll be all right, dear. Go back to sleep."

As Elizabeth and Daryl talked, Corinn moved slowly down the hall. Elizabeth waited to make sure Daryl wasn't getting up. Within seconds, she heard the regular breathing of one who is asleep. She followed Corinn.

When they got downstairs, they went out of the door and across the field to the barn. Elizabeth looked up at the stars. She picked the three brightest ones and made three wishes: for Daryl, for the runaways, and for herself.

Elizabeth and Corinn entered the barn. Inside they saw a small, tired looking woman standing with her feet planted apart and her head held up. Elizabeth could see the shiny barrel of a gun hanging down from the woman's hand. Elizabeth froze.

Corinn whispered to her, "Don't mind the gun, ma'am. Mrs. Tubman always carries one. It's just so she can protect herself."

"*Harriet* Tubman?" Elizabeth said too loudly.

"That's right," the small woman said. Her gaze was fixed on Elizabeth. Though the woman looked frail, her clear eyes showed she was in control. Harriet Tubman did not look like someone to cross. Elizabeth took a few steps back.

Sitting near the pile of hay were three more people, an elderly couple, and Jonathan.

"Jonathan?" Elizabeth said, looking to Corinn. Everything was becoming clear now. Corinn smiled.

"These are my parents," Jonathan said to

Elizabeth, waving to the old couple. "Mr. and Mrs. Bronson," he said, using their last name. This was not usually done in front of white people. Elizabeth saw that Jonathan was a proud man. That made her happy for Corinn, in spite of everything.

"Pleased to meet you." Elizabeth said. Jonathan stood and eyed her suspiciously. She could see that he did not trust her. And why should he? In a second, she could lose for him his parents, the woman he loved, and his own freedom. Elizabeth silently promised to do whatever was asked of her.

"No time for nice talk," Mrs. Tubman said. "You probably know that the slave catchers have had some success around here," she said to Elizabeth. "I'm proud to say that I've made more than a dozen trips on the underground railroad. And I've never lost a passenger. We must leave tomorrow. Those white men are probably moving from barn to farmhouse to barn looking for us. There is no time to lay over, even though these old people need some rest."

She pointed at Jonathan's parents. "I think we should move by the light of day tomorrow. People are less suspicious during the day."

"That's where you come in," Mrs. Tubman added, looking right at Elizabeth.

"What do I have to do?" Elizabeth asked.

"I want you to drive us to the next station tomorrow morning," Mrs. Tubman said. "It's twenty miles down the road in the town of Wilder, just across the McCall River. We will ride in the wagon under a load of hay."

"But people know me!" Elizabeth said. "It would look very strange for me to be driving a wagon."

"Can you handle a wagon and horse?" Mrs. Tubman asked.

"Well, yes," Elizabeth said. She thought back to her childhood on the farm. She had ridden better than her brothers much of the time. But that was years ago.

"You can dress as a boy so no one will know you," Mrs. Tubman said. "I've done it myself many times. I'd do it this time, but we need a white face."

Elizabeth looked at the runaways one by one. Mrs. Tubman, Corinn, Jonathan, and his parents. Slowly she nodded her head. She was ready for this job. Already she could feel the reins in her hands. And she could hear the heavy clop-clop of the horses' feet. They were keeping time with the beating of her heart.

CHAPTER

6

A Difficult Journey

The next morning Daryl left for work at his usual time, seven o'clock. As soon as he had gone, Elizabeth went to his room. She found an old pair of his trousers and tried them on. They were far too big.

She took out her sewing box and set to work. She only had about an hour-and-a-half to get ready. Harriet Tubman had said they would begin at 8.30.

When Elizabeth was finished, she pulled on the trousers. They fitted her fine. She found an old shirt that could pass for a boy's.

Then, she practised being a boy for a little while. First she walked around the room. She tried to let her arms and legs move loosely. Next she tried her voice. The first time she spoke, it sounded too low for a boy. She tried again, and felt that was better. She thought she could pass for a 14-year-old boy.

The last touch was to tie up her hair and put on a big straw hat. "Oh, no!" she cried into the mirror. Anyone could see that her long hair was pulled up under the hat.

There was only one thing she could do. And she only had a few moments to do it.

Elizabeth quickly found her sewing scissors. She took hold of the locks of hair that grew at the top of her neck. These were the ones that showed below the hat. She cut them to a length of one inch.

"There," she said, admiring her work. With the back of her hair cut short, no one would dream she was a woman. Then, later on, the rest of her hair would fall over the cut part. No one would ever know.

Elizabeth smiled. She was almost enjoying herself. If only she had David Sawyer's fake beard!

Now dressed completely in men's clothes, Elizabeth slipped downstairs. She would go out the back door where no one would see her. But just as she was shutting the door behind her, she heard something. It was the sound of voices in Corinn's cottage. Elizabeth knew it couldn't be the Bronsons. They would have stayed in the barn. She was sure of that. Elizabeth moved slowly and silently towards the cottage. She hid behind some bushes nearby and listened. She could hear the conversation clearly now.

One of the voices was Corinn's. And she sounded upset. The other voice was deep, but also a woman's. Elizabeth was afraid to admit to herself that that voice sounded familiar.

"I know you know where they are," the deep-voiced woman said. "I've seen you talking to Jonathan in town. I know there's something between you."

"I don't know what you're talking about," Corinn said.

"Yes you do," the woman said. "And I think you will tell me. If you don't, some unpleasant things could happen to you. *Very* unpleasant."

"I would help you if I could," Corinn answered calmly. "I have no idea where Jonathan is."

"I think you'll regret this, Corinn. And if you tell anyone about our conversation, you'll regret it even more."

Elizabeth crept quietly back to the house. She took off the boy's clothing and put on one of her own dresses. She brushed her long hair over the short back parts. Then she rushed back downstairs and out the back door.

"Corinn? Corinn?" she called. "Where are you?"

Corinn came out of the cottage followed by Martha Murphy.

"I'm sorry you had to find out this way," Martha said. "I thought Corinn and I could settle it ourselves. But since you are here, I must talk to you. I suppose it was my duty in the first place. Mr. Murphy caught Corinn stealing from the store in town. Didn't he, Corinn?"

"Yes, ma'am," Corinn lied.

"I came here to speak to her about it directly," said Martha, her nose sniffing the air.

Elizabeth swallowed a gasp. Sneaking around and lying like a thief. What had become of Martha? She used to be her friend.

Elizabeth followed Corinn's lead. They must both play the game very well now.

"Corinn," Elizabeth said as sternly as she could. "Wait in your cottage until I come to speak to you." Corinn went back into the cottage with her head down.

Martha trailed Elizabeth into the house.

"I'm so sorry to bring you this news. It's just awful, I know."

"You were only doing your duty, Martha," Elizabeth said.

Martha gave her old friend a questioning look. Then she put on a smile. "I must be going. By the way, did you hear that Jonathan from the Goodall's farm has run away?"

"No!" Elizabeth cried. Her hand flew to her throat.

"They've put up a $1500 reward for the return of him and his parents."

"Is that so?" Elizabeth said coolly. She noticed that Martha had on a new dress. She and Brian seemed to have come into a lot of money lately.

"As you know," Martha continued, "Brian has taken it to be his particular duty to look for runaways. He and his committee will have Jonathan by this afternoon. I'm sure of it. They can't have got too far yet. Why, I bet they are hiding within five miles of us right now." Martha smiled. "I must be off. Good day!"

Elizabeth raced upstairs to change back into the boy's clothes. She was late now. She wondered how much Martha knew. Perhaps she knew about the whole plan. Perhaps she was just playing cat and mouse with Elizabeth and Corinn. They must move – and move fast.

Elizabeth took one last look at herself in the mirror. She pulled a box out from under her bed. In the box she found a small gold bracelet. Her mother had given it to her when Elizabeth was twelve. As a child she had always believed it was magic, that it brought her good luck. Elizabeth slipped the bracelet in a pocket. She hurried towards the barn.

"Ready to go, Jumper?" Elizabeth said to the horse as she entered the barn. This sentence was the signal to the runaways that everything was clear.

First Jonathan crawled out from under the hay. Then came Harriet Tubman. They both helped Jonathan's parents out.

"Where's Corinn?" Jonathan asked nervously. "She was supposed to be here a while ago."

"She'll be here," Elizabeth answered. She didn't want to tell anyone what had happened with Martha. It would only make them more worried. Elizabeth hoped that Corinn was only waiting a little longer to make certain Martha didn't return.

"We won't leave without her," Jonathan said.

"We have to leave right away," Mrs. Tubman ordered.

"I won't go without Corinn," Jonathan started for the door.

"Get back here," cried Elizabeth. If one person spotted Jonathan, they were all dead. And there were spies everywhere.

Harriet Tubman lunged after Jonathan. The small woman looked as if she planned to wrestle the six-foot Jonathan to the ground.

Just in time, Corinn ran into the barn. Jonathan quickly hugged her. Mrs. Tubman grabbed and pushed the two of them towards the wagon.

Elizabeth took the pitchfork and threw some hay in the wagon bed. Jonathan helped his parents get in. Then he and Corinn climbed in. Mrs. Tubman and Elizabeth covered them with a huge pile of hay.

Elizabeth climbed into the driver's seat. "What about you?" she said to Mrs. Tubman.

"I'm not going," Mrs Tubman said. "I have some more work to do before heading back north. Thanks for the offer, anyway."

"You can't stay here," Elizabeth said.

"I won't be here much longer," Mrs. Tubman answered. "Now you must leave." Elizabeth nodded and shook the reins. They were on their way.

Once they were on the road, Elizabeth pressed Jumper to go faster. She enjoyed the feeling of sitting high on the wagon with the reins in her hands. She felt big and strong, like she had felt as a child racing her brothers.

Five miles out of town, Elizabeth heard the gallop of horses coming up behind her. She turned and saw two men riding to catch up with her. Suddenly she was frightened. Brian Murphy would surely recognize her, even in boy's clothes.

Elizabeth reached down to the floorboard. The wooden wagon was muddy. she wiped some dirt across her face. Anything to cover up as much as she could. The sound of galloping horses filled her ears.

"Morning, son!" The men on horses were beside her now. Elizabeth slowly turned to look at them. With relief, she didn't recognize either man.

"Morning," she said in a low voice.

"That hay must be as heavy as rocks at the speed you're going," the man said. He laughed and looked at his friend.

"Horses are lazy these days," the man said back. "Can't get them to work."

Elizabeth couldn't tell if they were suspicious of anything. Maybe they were just joking around.

The first man said, "We're looking for a runaway named Jonathan. He's about six feet tall. He's probably with two old people."

"Good luck to you," Elizabeth said. "I hope you find him. I haven't seen anyone like that on the road this morning."

"Brian Murphy said he might be running away with the Stellars' girl, Corinn. We were just at the Stellars' house. But all we found was an old black woman asleep in their barn.

Elizabeth felt her face get hot. "An old woman? What was she doing there?"

"I don't know," one of the men said. "The Stellars must have hired a little extra help. She looked so weak, though, she can't be much good to anyone. She jumped up and began pitching hay like crazy when we came in." The man threw back his head and laughed when he said this. "Scared of getting caught sleeping on the job, I guess."

"Guess so," Elizabeth said. "Just an old woman," Elizabeth thought. "Too weak to be much good to anyone!" This was not the first time Harriet Tubman had had the last laugh.

Elizabeth didn't think it would be the last time, either.

"Thanks anyway," the men said. "Have a good ride."

Elizabeth was so pleased with her acting, she began to tip her hat. Then she thought better of it. She could just see her long hair spilling down.

The men swung their horses around and rode back towards town. This was not a good sign. Surely the two men would report this conversation to someone. Elizabeth had no idea how much Martha Murphy knew. But she bet the "committee" was not finished checking out her house. The faster she went and the further away she got, the safer they would all be.

After about ten miles, the road entered the forest. Dark clouds began to fill the sky. Soon there was no blue showing at all. Elizabeth shivered. She had no jacket.

A few drops of rain began to fall. In minutes, it was raining hard. Elizabeth worried about Jonathan's parents. Because of their age, the rain and cold would bother them more. The horse slowed down, unwilling to go fast in the rain.

No one else was on the road. Elizabeth kept looking over her shoulder, expecting at any moment to see that she was being followed. She was relieved each time she saw the empty stretch of road behind her. Even so, she felt lonely. And she was shaking with cold.

Suddenly, a rider on a horse galloped out of the woods behind them. The rider was leaning forward and riding fast, trying to catch the wagon.

This was it. Elizabeth stood up and shook the reins. Jumper began to run. "Get up! Get up!" she cried to the horse.

But it was no use. The rider wasn't pulling a heavy wagon. In a few moments he was riding next to her.

"Look at me," the man shouted at her. The rain was beating down on her straw hat so loudly Elizabeth could hardly hear. She knew it was hopeless trying to get away from him, so she slowed down. Then she turned to face him.

The man had a full black beard. His hair was also black under his hat. But his eyes were sky blue. It was the minister, David Sawyer!

"Listen carefully," he said speaking as loudly as he could. "Murphy and his boys are on your trail. You spoke with two men who mentioned you to Murphy. He's riding out to check up on you. He and his friends will question you and probably search the wagon."

"They'll recognize me!"

"Yes," said Sawyer. "You must leave the wagon and horse. You'll have to go the last five miles on foot and through the woods. Stay off the road until you get to Wilder. Also, stay away from the bridge across the McCall River. It's watched 24 hours a day. Go at least a mile upriver and swim across."

"But I can't –"

"There's no time for talk now. Murphy and his boys are close behind. Do as I say. Here's a gun. If at any time someone stops you, say you are a slave catcher. Make up different names for the Bronsons and Corinn and say you are taking them to their owner in Wilder. I know you can do it. Be careful and God be with you. Go now."

Elizabeth jumped down from the driver's seat. Sawyer tied his horse in with Jumper. As he got in the driver's seat, the Bronsons and Corinn climbed out of the hay.

"Come on," Elizabeth said. "The longer we stay out here in the road, the greater the chances are that we'll be caught. The group of five hurried through the pounding rain into the darkness of the forest.

CHAPTER

7

Danger in the Woods

Everyone was wet and cold. It was nearly impossible to walk quickly through the woods. There were big logs to step over. As the five of them walked, their feet sank in the piles of soggy leaves. A wind blew the cold rain into their faces.

The group tried to keep the road in sight so they would not get lost. At the same time, they didn't want to be seen. It was important to blend in with the forest as much as squirrels did. The going was slow.

Mrs. Bronson began to have trouble keeping up. Corinn and Elizabeth each held one of the older woman's arms. Elizabeth thought her arm would break where the big woman hung onto it.

"What's that sound?" Jonathan said, and stopped walking. He reached for Corinn and pulled her to him. Elizabeth heard horses on the road. Then she could hear men's voices, too.

"I hear something," one of the men on the road said. "Over there in the woods."

Jonathan began sinking to his knees very slowly. He nodded for everyone to do the same. Without making a sound, they lowered themselves to the ground where they would be out of sight. The pounding of Elizabeth's heart sounded louder than a drumroll in her ears.

"Which way?" another man on the road asked. "We'll set the dogs loose."

"Forget it," said a voice that Elizabeth recognized. It was Brian Murphy. "They could never have walked this far by now. And the only wagon that has gone out on the road this morning was the one we checked. Let's head back to town. I bet they left by the southern road."

The sounds from the road faded into the distance. Murphy and his friends had turned back.

Jonathan bent over and lifted his mother. Elizabeth saw his face draw up in pain. He lifted the big woman on his back, placing her arms around his neck.

The group set out once more. Soon it became obvious that Mr. Bronson was also going to need help. Elizabeth and Corinn each put one of his arms around their own necks. He was much lighter than his wife. The two women were able to move him along, even if his feet had to drag a little.

As she moved slowly, sweating and gasping for air, Elizabeth felt she had been here before. The barking of dogs. The shouting of men's voices. The darkness of the forest.

Then she remembered her dream. This was it. The dream had told her of the work she would be called on to do. And deep inside herself she had known it all along.

Finally, the group reached the banks of the McCall River. They were just one mile above the bridge. Once they got across the river, they would be only one mile from the town of Wilder. There they would find safety.

The group stood for a minute and looked across to the other side of the muddy water. Suddenly, Corinn burst into tears. "Oh, Jonathan," she cried. "Not one of us can swim."

The river was moving quickly. Elizabeth knew the water was icy. A person could be swept away in a second.

"We will now," Jonathan said, his eyes fixed on the far bank. "Today we will learn to swim."

"Yes," said Elizabeth. She put an arm around Corinn. "Perhaps it's not too deep."

Elizabeth waited with Jonathan's parents as Jonathan and Corinn went first. They waded out slowly. Their clothes had already been soaked by the rain.

With each step, the water moved higher up on their bodies. Elizabeth knew the tug of the water was strong. Slowly, step by step, they went deeper. The water moved up around Jonathan's middle. He had a tight grip on Corinn's arm.

How much deeper would it get?

With the next few steps the water went back down to Jonathan's hips! they had been through the deepest part. Soon it was at his knees. Now they were on the far bank.

Elizabeth cried. Tears of joy washed down her face along with the rainwater. The river was not over their heads. They did not have to swim. Jonathan plunged into the river again, and waded back across quickly.

Elizabeth helped Mr. Bronson across as Jonathan helped his mother. Jonathan went back a last time for the gun. On the far bank they all hugged one another. Now, they had only to get through the streets of Wilder to the general store.

"Look mean," Jonathan said to Elizabeth with a grin. He handed her the gun. At first she looked at it in her hands as if it were a dead animal. Then she held it as she thought a man would. And they set off to walk into town.

When they reached Wilder, Elizabeth was surprised that they caught no one's eye. Then she realized that their wet clothes didn't give them away. It was still raining hard. Everyone in the streets was wet. On the far side of Main Street, Elizabeth spotted the general store.

"Ma'am!" Jonathan said to her. Elizabeth realized she had begun to break into a run. Never in her life had she wanted anything more than to be behind the doors of that store.

The others waited outside while Elizabeth went in. Behind the counter stood a tall thin man. He wore small glasses and had white hair. There were several customers in the store.

"May I help you?" asked the man.

"Yes." Elizabeth used her best boy's voice. "I have a delivery to make. Uh, the hay you asked for."

Saying this was part of her instructions. She realized now, though, that there was no wagon of hay outside. She hoped none of the customers would notice.

"Go around to the back," the man said. He smiled warmly, and pointed out of the door.

Elizabeth stepped back out in the rain. The Bronsons and Corinn were gone! She looked up and down the street. They had disappeared into thin air.

Something tugged at her shirt. Elizabeth looked down at a small boy, about eight years old. He said nothing to her. But he pulled at her shirt again. She followed him to the back of the store.

There he took her into what looked like a woodshed. Behind a small pile of wood, though, was another door. This led to a secret room at the back of the store.

The silent boy pushed her in and slipped in after her.

Before Elizabeth was the most welcome sight in her life. The runaways were already seated at a big table. A small fire was crackling in a fireplace. Elizabeth saw that the fireplace shared a chimney with the one in the store.

"You must be Mrs. Stellar," said a woman with a kind face. "I am Mrs. Oakley. Thank goodness you are all safe. Sit down."

Mrs. Oakley had a hot meal ready for them in no time. Elizabeth and the others fell on the food like vultures. Without a word they ate and drank. When a plate was empty, Mrs. Oakley filled it. Knowing how tired and hungry they were, she asked no questions.

Soon Mr. Oakley, the man in the store, slipped into the room. "Welcome to the Wilder station of the underground railroad," he said. "You are safe here. We have beds for you to sleep on. Later, we will talk about the next leg of your journey."

Elizabeth saw Corinn nod silently. She and Jonathan had not let go of each other's hands since they arrived at the Oakley's.

"I understand that you must get home before your husband tonight, Mrs. Stellar," Mr. Oakley said. "My grandson's saddled a fresh horse ready for you. Someone will come to get it from your barn tonight."

"You had better hurry," Mrs Oakley said. "I wish I had dry clothes I could give you. But here, take this jacket." Elizabeth put on the man's jacket. It was too big, but it was warm.

"I would like to talk to Corrin alone for a minute," Elizabeth said before she left. She looked around the room. It was too small for a private conversation. So she went ahead and said, "I just wanted to wish you and Jonathan much happiness."

Corinn nodded and answered, "Thank you, ma'am. We will never forget what you have done for us."

Elizabeth reached in her pocket. She pulled out the gold bracelet. "I'd like you to have this. For good luck. Goodbye."

When Elizabeth went outside, she was pleased to see that the rain had stopped. She was able to ride hard all the way back to her farm. She arrived home just minutes before Daryl was expected. She put her horse in the barn. Then she ran across the wet field towards the warm house and dry clothes.

Home! As Elizabeth went in the back door she wanted to cry out in joy. By the time Daryl got home she would be all cleaned up and have on a dress. She began to climb the stairs to her bedroom. At the top of the stairs she suddenly realized how tired she was.

"What are you doing!" a man shouted.

Elizabeth whirled around. Daryl was

standing at the bottom of the long flight of stairs.

"Don't move," he said. His face was filled with anger. He moved slowly up the stairs towards her. "I'm going to check your pockets and then take you to the police."

Elizabeth realized Daryl didn't recognize her. Only her cut hair showed under the big straw hat. She still had mud all over her face. And she was wearing the heavy man's jacket Mrs. Oakley had given her. Elizabeth had to think fast now. If Daryl got any closer, he would recognize her. Elizabeth knew Daryl didn't keep a gun in the house. She would have a chance if she ran. She turned and took off towards the back bedroom. She opened the door to the servant's stairs. Down she flew. Daryl was close on her heels shouting, "Thief! Thief!"

At the bottom of the servant's stairs Elizabeth slammed the door shut. She raced out the back door and slammed that behind her, too. She knew the back garden much better than Daryl. She went to a far corner where she had not yet done any work. The bushes were thick. Elizabeth climbed in behind them.

She got there just in time. Daryl came running out the back door. Elizabeth lay as still as she could. She held her breath. Instead of searching the garden, Daryl ran out in the road.

Minutes later, he was back. He was talking to himself, angrily. She knew he would search the house for anything missing. Then he would go to the police. That's when she could get back in the house.

Elizabeth was terribly cold. She lay in the bushes wondering about her life. Chased like a thief by her own husband! Would life ever be normal for them again? Would she ever be able to tell him what she had done?

It seemed that hours had passed when Elizabeth heard Daryl finally leave the house. It had probably only been a few minutes. She crawled out of the bushes and crept inside.

Elizabeth threw off the boy's clothes and hid them. Then she washed and got into bed. Daryl had not discovered her. Yet.

CHAPTER

8

The Truth Comes Out

The next morning Elizabeth did not get out of bed. She had a bad cold and a high fever.

"I've been worried you would get sick," Daryl said to her. "It's my fault. I've been away from home so much." He said nothing about the thief. Nor did he ask where she had been in the early evening when he had come home yesterday.

"I've missed you," Elizabeth said. Her head was completely stuffed up and she was still very tired.

"Where is Corinn?" Daryl asked. "I'll have her make you some tea."

"I'm not sure exactly where she is." Elizabeth answered.

"I'll get her."

As Daryl started downstairs, Elizabeth heard someone knocking on the door. When

Daryl answered it, she heard Priscilla's voice.

"Oh! I heard the news!" Priscilla sang out in her high voice.

"What news?" asked Daryl.

"What news! About Corinn, of course. What are you going to do? Is Elizabeth *very* upset? I just can't imagine how Corinn slipped out under your very eyes. I mean, really –"

"Hold on, hold on," Daryl said. "What in the world are you talking about?"

As Elizabeth lay in bed she could just picture Priscilla's eyes getting wide.

"You don't know?" Priscilla squealed. "Why, Martha Murphy said she knows for a fact that Corinn ran away with Jonathan from the Goodall's farm. Go look for yourself. Corinn is not out in the cottage."

"Well, good morning!" This time Elizabeth recognized Martha's voice. "It is my duty to tell you, Daryl, that Corinn has run away. When Brian couldn't find Jonathan yesterday, I came looking for you and Elizabeth. I couldn't find either of you. So I searched Corinn's cottage, and she was gone! She must have run away with Jonathan while you two were out yesterday. I am sorry to be the one to bring you this news."

That was the last thing Elizabeth heard before she passed out. The next thing she knew, she was bathed in sweat and Daryl was wiping her face with a cold cloth.

Later, when Elizabeth felt a little better, Daryl told her what Priscilla and Martha had had to say. He sighed deeply as he sat on the edge of her bed.

"Martha wanted to know how much money we will give for her return," Daryl said.

"Oh, we won't do that, will we?" Elizabeth asked.

"No," Daryl said quietly. "The Goodalls are making enough of a scene about Jonathan and his parents. The important thing for us now is that you get well."

Elizabeth stayed in bed for a week. She would not see any visitors. Most people in town thought she was upset about Corinn's running away. When she showed herself in town again, people whispered quietly as she passed. But no one questioned her about Corinn.

While Elizabeth was sick in bed, Daryl had been very sweet and attentive. It was almost like old times. Elizabeth had decided she could no longer live with her lie. She had to tell Daryl everything. War between the North and South was almost certain now. The time had come to take sides, and she knew where she stood.

Two weeks after Elizabeth's journey to Wilder, there was another abolitionist meeting. She wanted to go. She would talk to Daryl first, though. She would tell him everything.

That night they sat down to dinner. Daryl was acting strangely again, as if his thoughts were far away.

"Daryl," Elizabeth began. "I must tell you something very important."

"Yes, dear?" Daryl did not look at her. He was eating his chicken quickly.

"It is about Corinn."

"I know. You need some help. Of course you can't do all the work."

"No, it's not that. I'm happy doing the work."

"Can we talk later?" Daryl got up and pushed in his chair. "I have a meeting."

"Daryl!" Elizabeth jumped up to face him. "Can't we ever talk?" Her eyes filled with tears.

"I'm sorry," he said. "First thing in the morning, all right?"

"Fine," Elizabeth said, her voice cracking. "In the morning."

Daryl left and Elizabeth did the dishes quickly. She had a meeting tonight herself. If her marriage was going to fall apart at least she would have her work. She knew Ann would always be there for her, too.

Elizabeth entered the store where the secret meeting was being held. So far she had only gone to the two public meetings. Now she was being asked to the secret ones where the real planning was done. The room was packed. There were both black and white people there.

Since the meeting hadn't started, people were talking in small groups. Elizabeth found Ann near the door and fell into her arms. "Oh, Elizabeth," Ann cried. "I heard what you did, though I wasn't supposed to know. I'm so proud of you. You are the bravest woman I know."

"Was it you who put them up to asking me?" Elizabeth asked. She was still a little angry about that part.

"No. You should know I wouldn't do that. The only thing I did was answer 'yes' when David Sawyer asked if you were to be trusted. I didn't know for what. Until later."

"Then it was Corinn?"

Ann nodded. "She knew where your heart lay."

"My heart also lies with my husband," Elizabeth said. Then she couldn't stop the tears. They overflowed. A few people near them turned and stared.

"But Elizabeth!" Ann took her friend by the shoulders. "Surely you know!"

"Know what?" Elizabeth asked, her voice husky with crying. She looked up at Ann and was surprised to see her friend laughing.

"Oh, my, we are *too* good at keeping secrets! Come with me, Elizabeth." Ann led Elizabeth through the crowd. "I have someone I want you to meet."

The next time Elizabeth looked up she was looking into the surprised face of her own husband. "Daryl?" she whispered. "What are you doing here?"

"What are *you* doing here?" he shot back.

"I thought you two had come together!" Ann said.

Elizabeth and Daryl stared at each other in disbelief. Then Daryl took her hand and led her through the people to the door. Outside on the street they stared at each other silently for several moments.

Finally, a smile appeared at the corner of Elizabeth's mouth. "Is this why . . .?" she began.

"I'm beginning to understand quite a bit, I think," Daryl said.

Elizabeth laughed. "Oh, I think there is probably quite a bit you don't understand!" She thought of the runaways in the barn, her journey, Daryl chasing her.

"We have a lot to talk about," Daryl said.

"I tried to talk this evening."

Daryl lowered his head. "I'm sorry. I have been so afraid to tell you what was on my mind. This abolitionist work means the end of my job, you know. It may mean selling our home, a complete change in our lives. I was so afraid you would never understand. I hardly understand it myself! How will we live?"

Elizabeth smiled once more. Her future had never been more uncertain. Yet her heart had never been lighter. She took Daryl's hand and pulled him towards home. They could miss this meeting tonight. There would be many more. For now, they had a lot of catching up to do.